You Can Win a Prize!

By Clem King

You can win a prize,
like these kids.

And you can just have fun
while you play games!

Kate can win a prize
while she rides her bike.

Jane can win a prize for skate tricks.

She is good,
and she is safe!

Miles can use his kite to do tricks.

He grabs the rope and runs.

He wins the top prize!

June hangs from soft ropes to win a prize.

She makes shapes.

Rose slides in to home base and wins the game.

She and her mates win the prize!

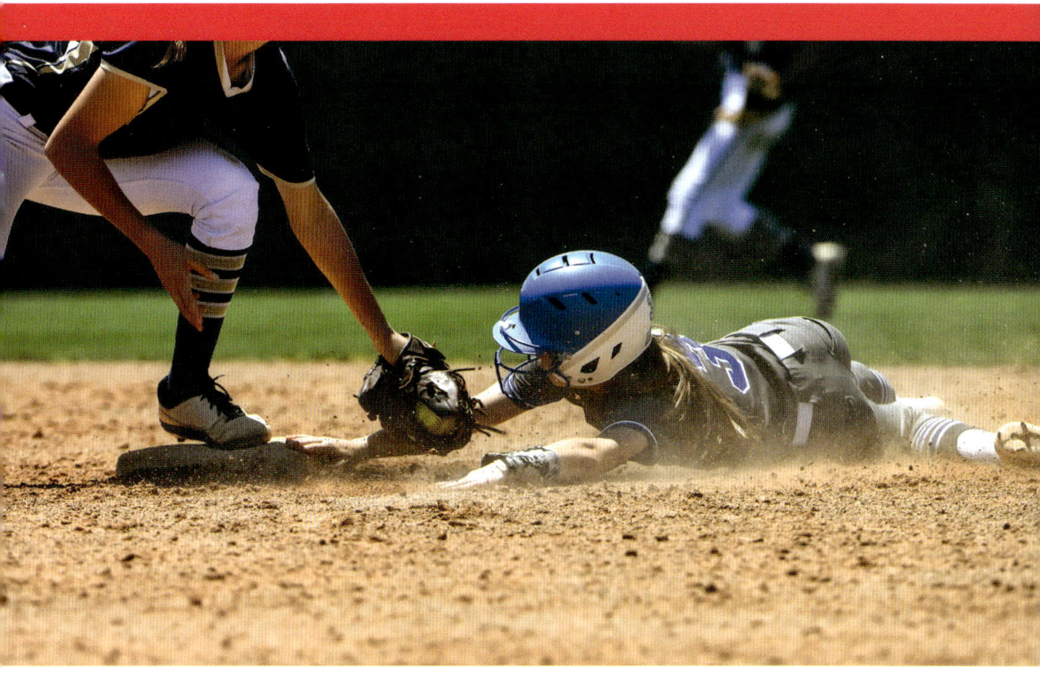

If Pete is quick when he runs, he can win a prize.

Chase those kids to the line, Pete!

You can win a prize.

And you can just take your time while you have fun!

CHECKING FOR MEANING

1. What does Jane win a prize for? *(Literal)*
2. Which prize does Miles win? *(Literal)*
3. Why do you think Miles grabs the rope and runs before doing kite tricks? *(Inferential)*

EXTENDING VOCABULARY

prize	What sounds are in the word *prize*? What does it mean if you win a prize?
skate	In the text, Jane does skate tricks. What does the word *skate* mean? Jane uses a skateboard to do her tricks. What are some other types of skating?
chase	What does the word *chase* mean? When might you chase someone?

MOVING BEYOND THE TEXT

1. Why is it important to have a good attitude when you **don't** win a prize? Why is it important to be kind when you do win?
2. When have you been proud of something that you have done?
3. Why is it also important to just have fun when you play sports or do tricks?
4. What are some activities that you do well?

TIME TO WRITE

Write about something you are good at!

PRACTICE WORDS